TODAY WAS MY FIRST VIOLA LESSON

WRITTEN AND ILLUSTRATED BY RAFAEL RAMIREZ
DIGITALIZED BY NORMAN BERMUDEZ
EDITED BY MARIA A. BERMUDEZ

©2014 Rafael Ramirez

Hi, my name is Mia.

Today was my first viola lesson.

My Mom told me that I will learn how to play the viola.

We went to my teacher's Viola Studio.

Mr. Ramirez is my viola teacher.

My teacher told me about
the different parts of the viola...

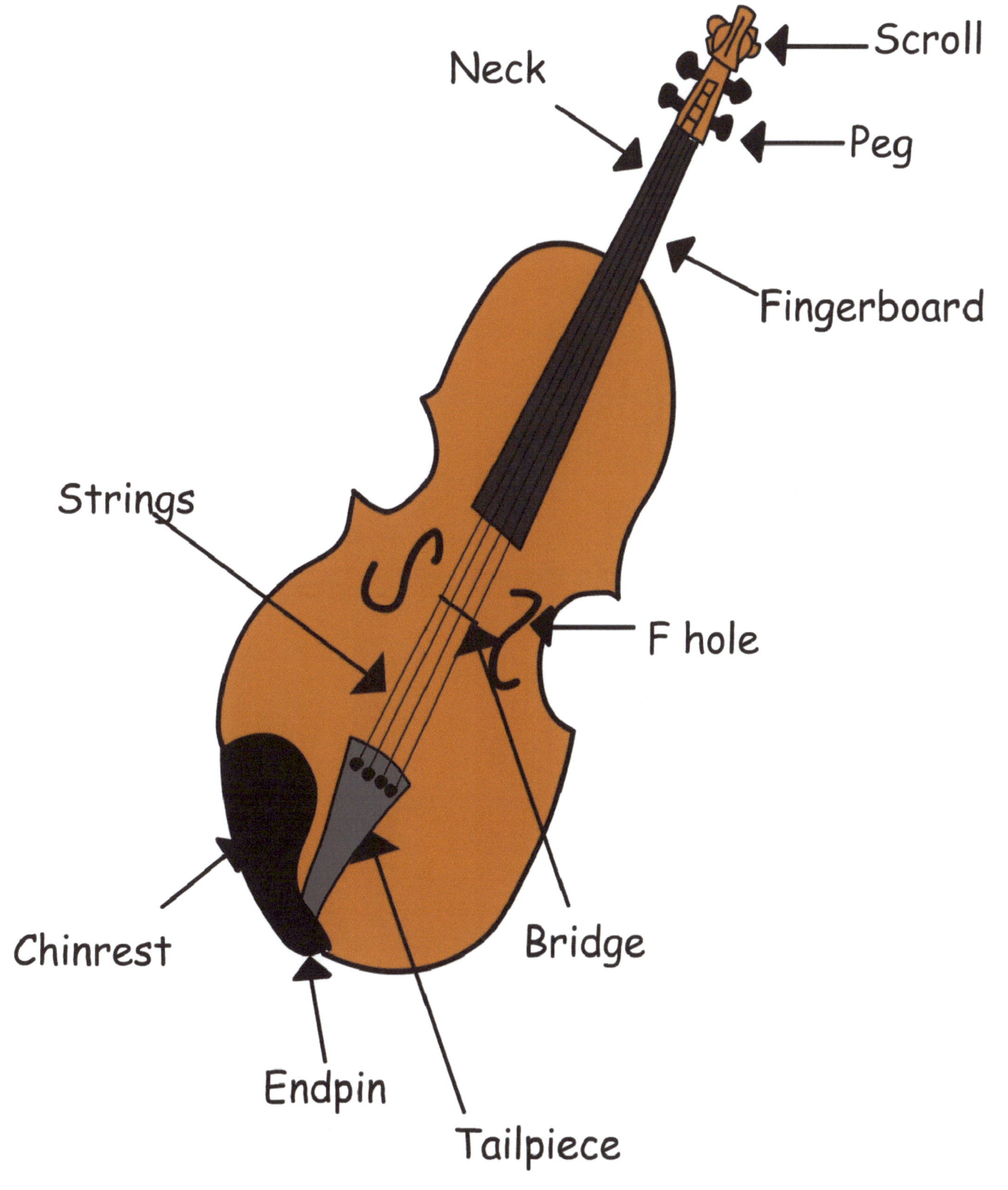

...And

the parts of the bow.

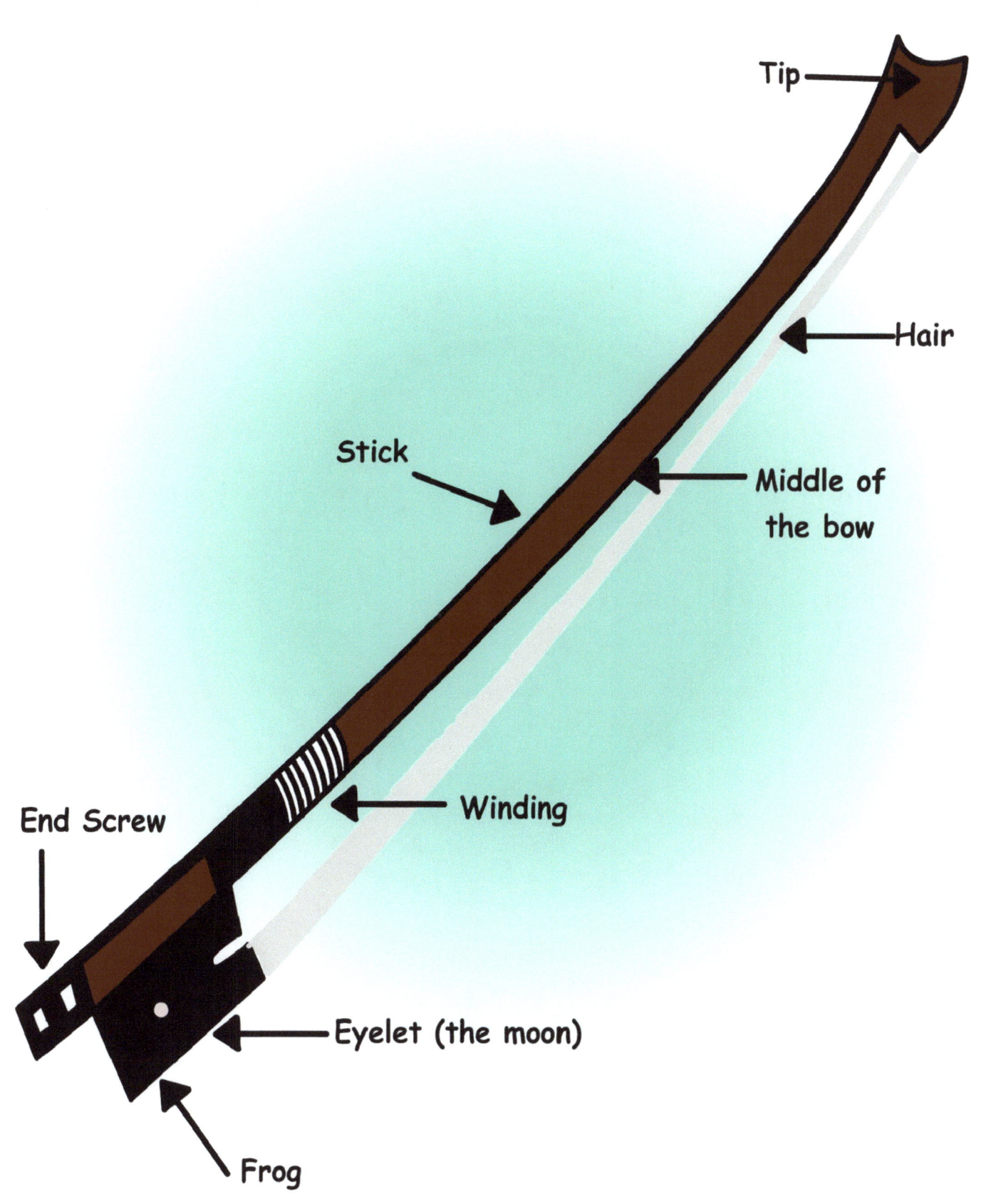

I need to practice how to hold the bow. This will help me make a beautiful sound.

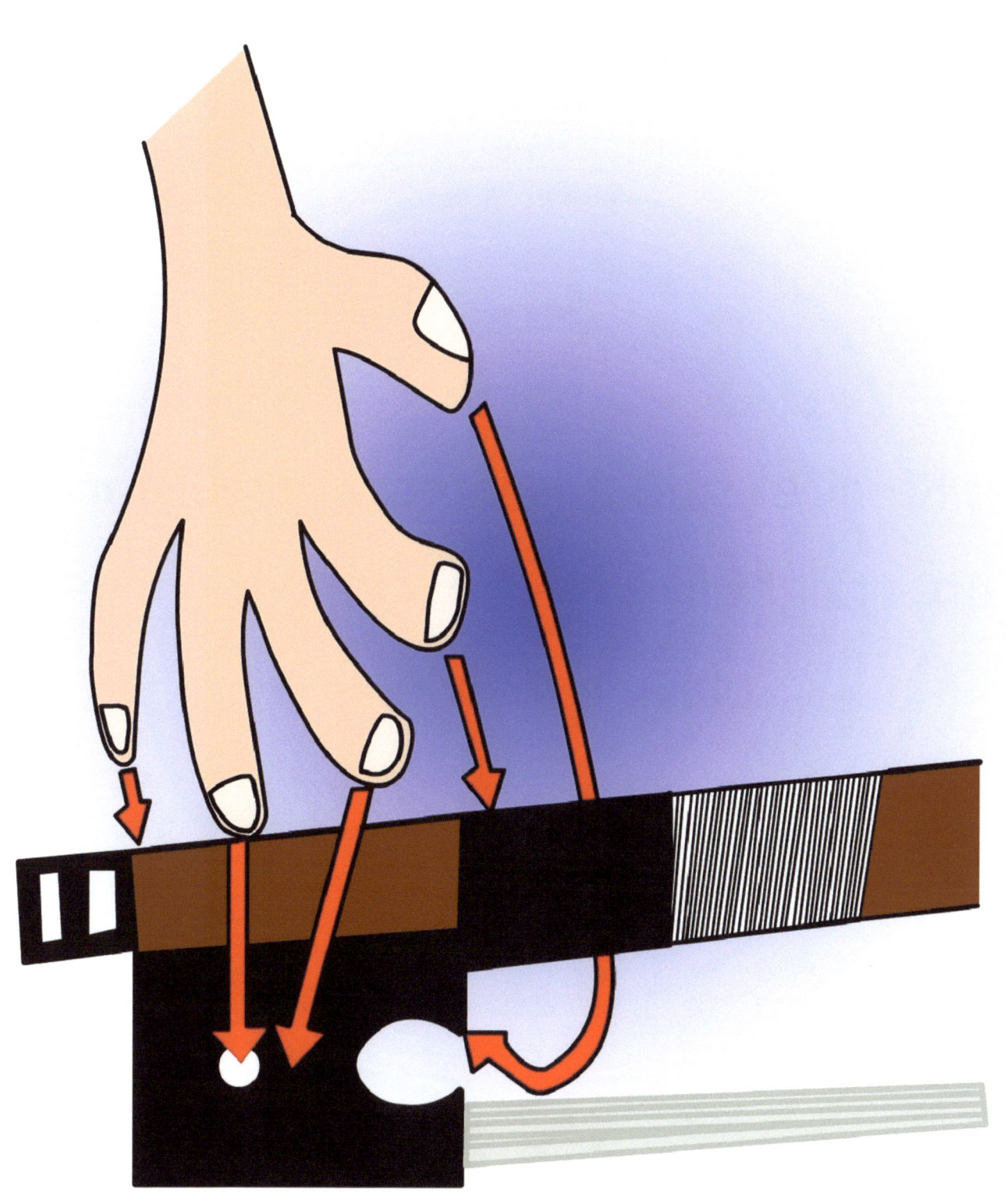

Mr. Ramirez said it is important to stand up straight like the bow knight while playing my viola.

I learned how to do down bow (Π)...

...and up bow (V).

Mr. Ramirez said:

"The bow has to go straight like a train to make a beautiful sound."

I learned about:

The music staff. It is used to notate music.

The pitches – The musical notes, and the type of notes.

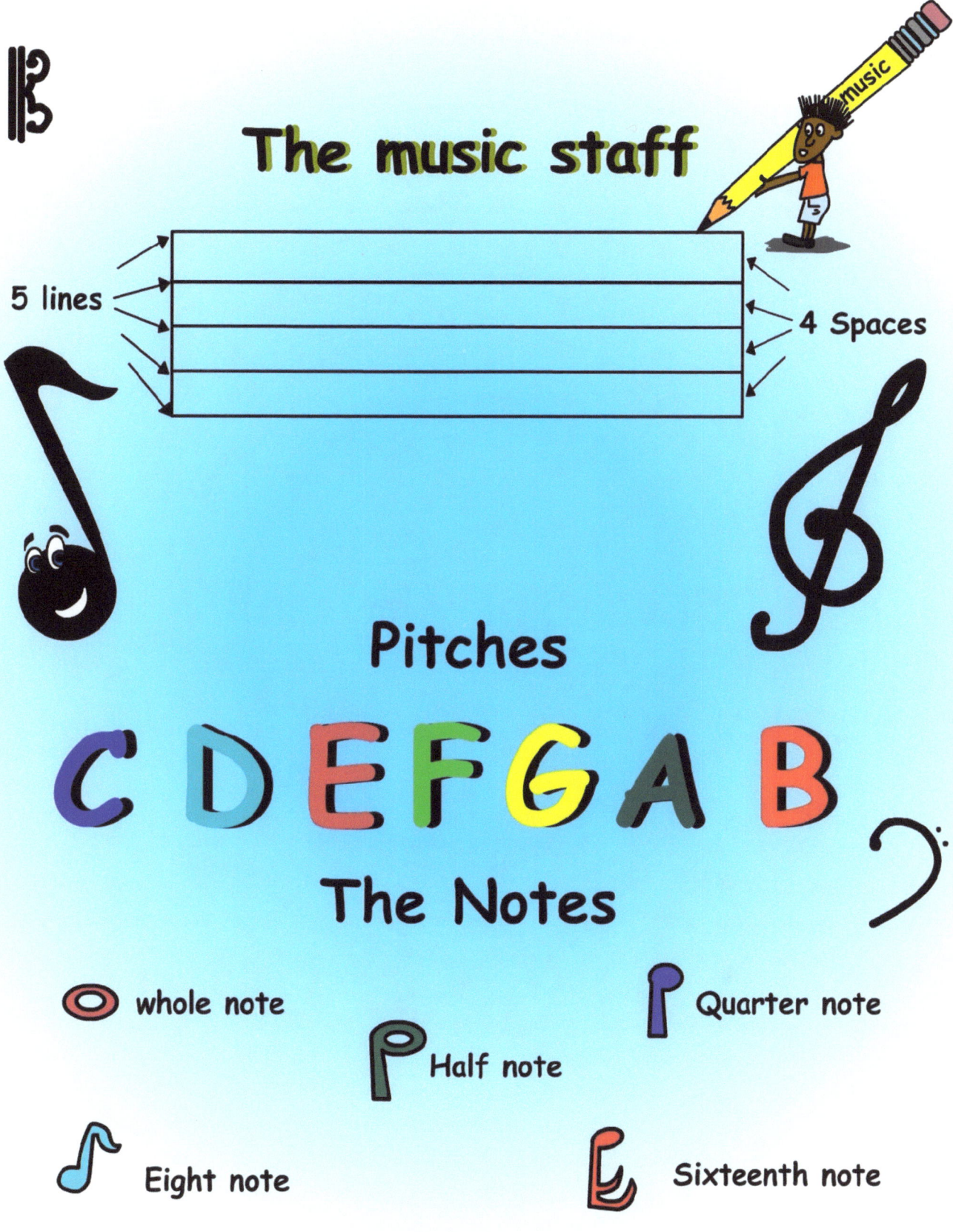

I love to play my viola.

My teacher surprised me at the end of the lesson with a piece of candy and my first viola book.

I love my viola lessons.

www.ingramcontent.com/pod-product-compliance
Lightning Source LLC
Chambersburg PA
CBHW041231040426
42444CB00002B/122